OUT AND ABOUT
MINIBEAST
EXPLORER

A children's guide to over
60 different minibeasts

First published in the United Kingdom in 2018 by Nosy Crow Ltd
The Crow's Nest, 14 Baden Place, Crosby Row
London SE1 1YW
www.nosycrow.com

This edition published 2021

ISBN 978 1 78800 441 1

Text by Robyn Swift 2018
Text © Nosy Crow 2018
Illustrations © Hannah Alice 2018

The right of Robyn Swift to be identified as the author and Hannah
Alice to be identified as the illustrator of this work has been asserted.

A CIP catalogue record for this book is available from
the British Library.

Printed in China

Papers used by Nosy Crow are made from
wood grown in sustainable forests.

3 5 7 9 8 6 4

CONTENTS

WHAT ARE MINIBEASTS?

Have you ever looked under a log to see what might be living there? Or what about taking a closer look among the leaves or deep in the soil in your garden? Wherever you live and whatever the weather, if you look hard enough, you are likely to see a minibeast.

CINNABAR MOTH

BUMBLEBEE

ANT

Minibeasts are tiny little creatures without a backbone. This means that some minibeasts, like wriggly worms, have soft, bendy bodies; and some minibeasts, like spiders, have a hard shell on the outside of their body instead of a backbone. This is called an exoskeleton.

EMPEROR MOTH CATERPILLAR

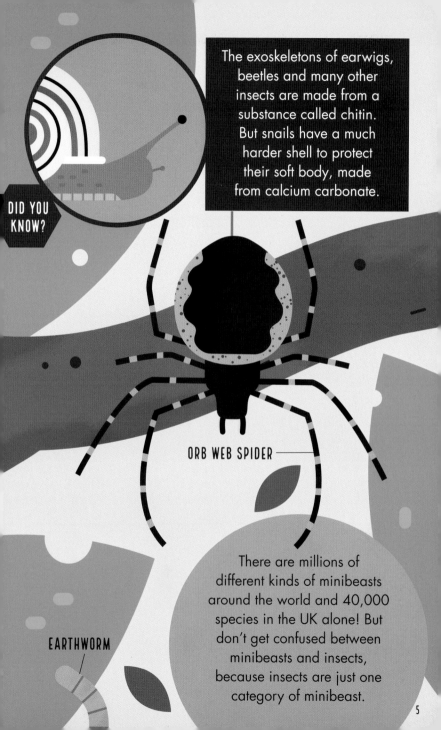

DID YOU KNOW?

The exoskeletons of earwigs, beetles and many other insects are made from a substance called chitin. But snails have a much harder shell to protect their soft body, made from calcium carbonate.

ORB WEB SPIDER

EARTHWORM

There are millions of different kinds of minibeasts around the world and 40,000 species in the UK alone! But don't get confused between minibeasts and insects, because insects are just one category of minibeast.

5

ANATOMY

Insects have a three-part body with a head, thorax and abdomen. They usually have wings so that they can fly.

Most insects have eyes made up of many small lenses.

An insect's head contains the sensory organs, such as eyes, antennae and mouthparts.

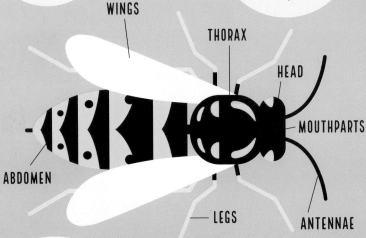

WINGS

THORAX

HEAD

MOUTHPARTS

ABDOMEN

LEGS

ANTENNAE

Three pairs of legs are attached to the thorax (the middle part of the body), and if an insect has wings, they're attached to the thorax, too.

The antennae are used to sense smell, touch and sound; and the mouthparts are used for different ways of feeding, such as chewing, biting, stabbing and sucking.

If you find a minibeast and would like to identify it, the best starting point is to count up how many legs it has. This will also help you discover whether it is an insect or not.

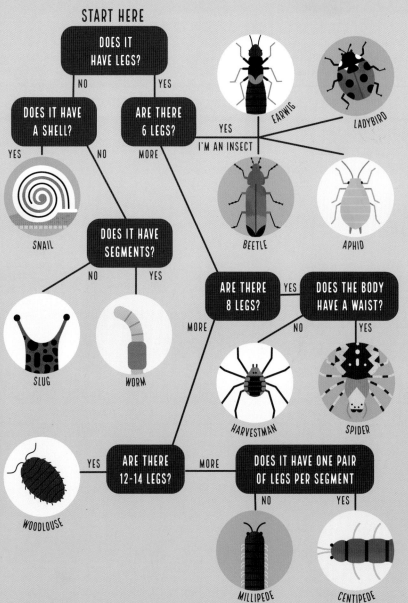

START HERE

DOES IT HAVE LEGS?

NO

DOES IT HAVE A SHELL?

YES

ARE THERE 6 LEGS?

YES

EARWIG

LADYBIRD

YES
I'M AN INSECT

MORE

BEETLE

APHID

YES

SNAIL

NO

NO

DOES IT HAVE SEGMENTS?

NO

YES

SLUG

WORM

ARE THERE 8 LEGS?

YES

DOES THE BODY HAVE A WAIST?

NO

YES

MORE

HARVESTMAN

SPIDER

YES

WOODLOUSE

ARE THERE 12-14 LEGS?

MORE

DOES IT HAVE ONE PAIR OF LEGS PER SEGMENT

NO

YES

MILLIPEDE

CENTIPEDE

TOP TIPS

There are some important things to remember
when you're looking for minibeasts so that
you don't harm them (or yourself!).

Because minibeasts are so tiny, you'll need to get up
close to see how they work. For this, you will need to
look through a minibeast magnifier which will usually
enlarge the creature by about two or three times –
enough to see a lot of extra detail. But to get an even
closer look, a hand-held magnifying lens is best, as
they tend to enlarge things by about 10 times.

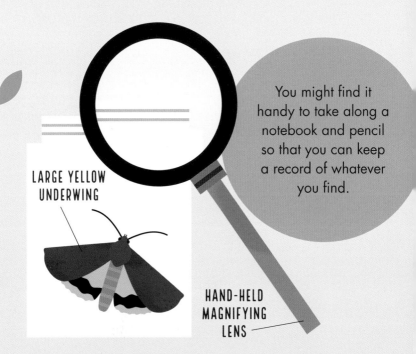

You might find it
handy to take along a
notebook and pencil
so that you can keep
a record of whatever
you find.

LARGE YELLOW
UNDERWING

HAND-HELD
MAGNIFYING
LENS

1. You'll need a container to store each minibeast in. Either jam jars or clean, empty plastic tubs make good containers for living minibeasts.

Make sure there are air holes in the lid (you could use a drawing pin to make tiny holes) and add some kitchen roll as padding.

— TWEEZERS

2. Never touch a bug with your bare hands, unless you know that it is harmless. It's a good idea to take tweezers so you can carefully pick up any minibeasts you find and a soft brush so you can gently nudge them to see how they move.

3. Remember to always release minibeasts back where you found them after you have finished looking at them.

4. It's best to lift up stones or branches carefully with a stick first, because sometimes minibeasts can bite or sting.

Always take an adult with you if you're going exploring at night.

WHERE DO MINIBEASTS LIVE?

You'll find minibeasts living in land, air or water. In fact, the only place minibeasts can't survive is in the very coldest places in the world. They find somewhere which gives them everything they need to survive – food, water and shelter. This place is called a habitat.

Minibeasts like woodlice, centipedes, millipedes and beetles love dark and damp surroundings.

CLICK BEETLE

A habitat can be as big as a forest or as small as a leaf. One of the best places to discover minibeasts is in leaf litter, which is the leaves, twigs and bark that have fallen to the ground and started to rot.

Many minibeasts, such as caterpillars and aphids, live in trees and shrubs because there is plenty there for them to eat. They are also well camouflaged so that they can hide away from birds that might want to eat them.

SWALLOWTAIL CATERPILLAR

On warm sunny days you'll see insects like butterflies and bees in the grass, as they visit flowers to get their food. You might also spot spiders as they like hiding out in grassy places and under stones.

MONARCH
BUTTERFLY

Some minibeasts even live inside our houses. Sometimes flies and mosquitoes fly in through open doors and windows, and spiders often hide in dark, quiet corners.

GARDEN
SPIDER

HOUSEFLY   DRAGONFLY

Lots of minibeasts live in freshwater, so there's plenty to see in ponds and streams. Some live on the surface of the water and some swim underneath. You might also see flying insects like dragonflies speeding through the air.

Look out for spiders in the bathroom, too – sometimes they get stuck in the bath or sink because they can't climb up the slippery sides!

11

WHAT DO MINIBEASTS EAT?

Many minibeasts only eat plants, which means they are called herbivores. They usually enjoy leaves in particular, but some feed on fruit, nectar and pollen. Herbivores have to watch out for minibeasts that eat other creatures – these are called carnivores and they can be powerful and ferocious.

HERBIVORES

Insects like grasshoppers and caterpillars have special mouthparts which can grind up tough green leaves. Slugs and snails have a special tongue called a radula, which is a bit like a conveyor belt covered in tiny teeth that tears up plant food.

GRASSHOPPERS AND CATERPILLARS

APHIDS

Insects like aphids have special mouthparts that can pierce a plant stem and suck up the sap and nectar from inside.

BUTTERFLIES AND MOTHS

Butterflies and moths have a long thin tongue for sucking up the nectar from flowers or rotting fruit.

CARNIVORES

Spiders will hunt or trap their prey using webs, and beetles use their long legs to run fast and hunt for food at night. They have sharp jaws so they can eat other minibeasts.

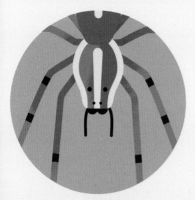

SPIDERS

Some minibeasts, such as ants, flies and wasps, eat both plants and other creatures and are called omnivores.

Larger carnivores like birds, lizards, weasels, badgers and foxes love eating minibeasts. When a herbivore eats a plant, then a carnivore eats the herbivore, this is called a food chain, and every animal is a link in the chain.

DID YOU KNOW?

FOOD CHAIN

OAK LEAF

CATERPILLAR

SOLDIER BEETLE

SHREW

FOX

13

MINIBEASTS IN THE AIR

LADYBIRD IN FLIGHT

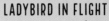

Sometimes minibeasts are called creepy-crawlies because of the way they crawl and scuttle along the ground, but many insects also have wings so they can fly through the air.

MAGNIFY THIS!

Not all insects' wings are the same. Take a closer look to see that a fly has just two wings, whereas most insects have four.

14

If you look closely at a lacewing's wing, you'll see a network of criss-crossing veins. These strengthen the wings and help them to keep their shape as they beat up and down.

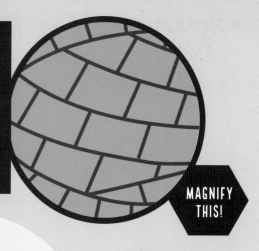

MAGNIFY THIS!

Beetles have extra strong front wings that cover their delicate hindwings like a case, so that they don't get damaged as they crawl around. This means it takes them a few seconds to get their wings ready before they can take off, so they often decide to walk away from hungry predators instead.

CLICK BEETLE

HOUSEFLY

Unlike beetles, flies can take off almost instantly which is why they are so tricky to swat if they are buzzing around the house.

MINIBEASTS AT NIGHT

There are just as many minibeasts that come out at night as there are during the daytime. You just need to know how to find them! You'll see many nocturnal minibeasts when looking under rocks and logs where it's dark, but some are so secretive that you'll only find them if you go out at night with a torch.

One easy way to catch these nocturnal creepy-crawlies is to set up a simple pitfall trap overnight. You can then visit your trap during the day to examine the minibeasts more closely.

To increase your chances of catching some interesting minibeasts, you could set up several traps in different areas around your garden.

1. Dig a small hole in soft ground and bury a plastic cup up to the rim.

2. Add some dry leaves to the bottom of the cup for minibeasts to hide in. You could also add some food to attract them – meat, cheese or fruit is good.

3. Put stones on the ground around the cup and place a tile or piece of wood over the top. This will protect the trap from rain.

4. Leave the trap overnight and check the next morning for any animal that may have fallen in during the night.

5. Take a closer look at whatever you've caught using a magnifying glass and remember to release them once you're done.

ANT

WOODLOUSE

MINIBEASTS AND FLOWERS

The biggest group of minibeasts – insects – will often be found flitting around the flowers in your garden. Flowers are designed specifically to attract insects because they contain food called nectar, a sugary liquid packed with energy. Some insects also use flowers as meeting places or even traps so they can catch and eat other insects.

HOVERFLY

Insects help flowers too, as they spread pollen from flower to flower and help plants to make their seeds.

Insects like flies and beetles are attracted to flowers with an open, flat structure, so that they can easily reach the nectar inside without needing a special long tongue. Flies are attracted to strong-smelling flowers – even those that we don't think smell very nice.

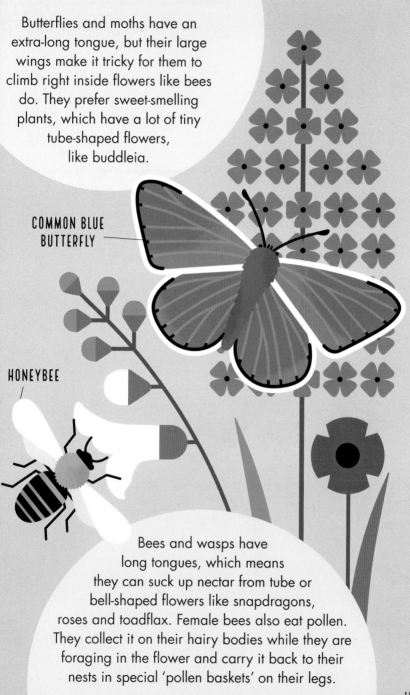

Butterflies and moths have an extra-long tongue, but their large wings make it tricky for them to climb right inside flowers like bees do. They prefer sweet-smelling plants, which have a lot of tiny tube-shaped flowers, like buddleia.

COMMON BLUE BUTTERFLY

HONEYBEE

Bees and wasps have long tongues, which means they can suck up nectar from tube or bell-shaped flowers like snapdragons, roses and toadflax. Female bees also eat pollen. They collect it on their hairy bodies while they are foraging in the flower and carry it back to their nests in special 'pollen baskets' on their legs.

MINIBEASTS THROUGH THE YEAR

All minibeasts are cold-blooded, which means they cannot keep themselves warm like we do. Instead, they get their body heat from the sun. You'll find minibeasts soaking up the sunshine in warm spots around the garden, on rocks or logs on the ground or on the tops of plants.

Butterflies open up their wings while they're sunbathing to collect as much warmth as they can. You'll most likely find this happening early in the morning as they're warming up for the day ahead.

PAINTED LADY BUTTERFLY

In hot temperatures, insects also grow more quickly and their life cycles speed up. This is why summer is the busiest time for minibeasts.

Warmth makes insects move faster, which makes them more difficult to catch, and if it gets too cold, they slow down – sometimes even coming to a complete stop.

Most minibeasts hibernate through the winter as they wait for the warmer weather to return, or they spend the cold months as eggs or pupae. They choose to stay in warm, sheltered places like compost heaps and log piles, but you can help them by making your own hibernation home.

It can be as big or small as you like, just make sure there are lots of little spaces for the minibeasts to crawl into.

You can use bricks, dead wood, bamboo, flowerpots filled with hay or straw – anything that creates a lot of nooks and crannies.

BUTTERFLY LIFE CYCLE

The life cycle of a butterfly has four main parts:
egg, caterpillar, pupa and butterfly or moth.

1 All butterflies start life as an egg. Butterflies stick their eggs on to leaves so baby caterpillars can starting eating food as soon as they hatch.

EGG

PEACOCK CATERPILLAR

2 Caterpillars get bigger and bigger by eating lots of leaves.

3 A caterpillar sheds its outer skin several times, usually dropping the old, empty skin on the ground.

OLD SKIN

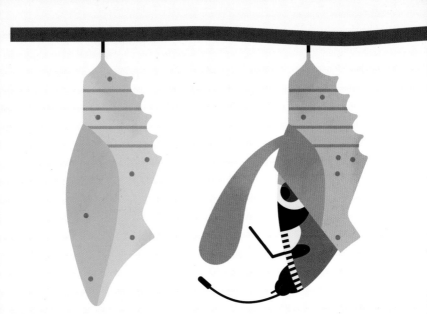

4 The caterpillar's skin becomes a shell and inside the caterpillar turns into a pupa (or chrysalis).

5 After about two weeks, the pupa splits open and an adult butterfly or moth crawls out.

PEACOCK BUTTERFLY

6 Once its wings have hardened, it can fly away.

CATERPILLARS

Caterpillars are baby butterflies or moths and they can be lots of different colours, but they are usually the same colour as their habitat. This is called camouflage and helps them to blend in so they don't get eaten by birds or wasps.

Sometimes if you look closely at leaves, you can see little holes where caterpillars have munched their way through.

MAGNIFY THIS!

SWALLOWTAIL CATERPILLAR

CABBAGE WHITE CATERPILLAR

As well as camouflage, some caterpillars can produce a foul smell to keep predators away.

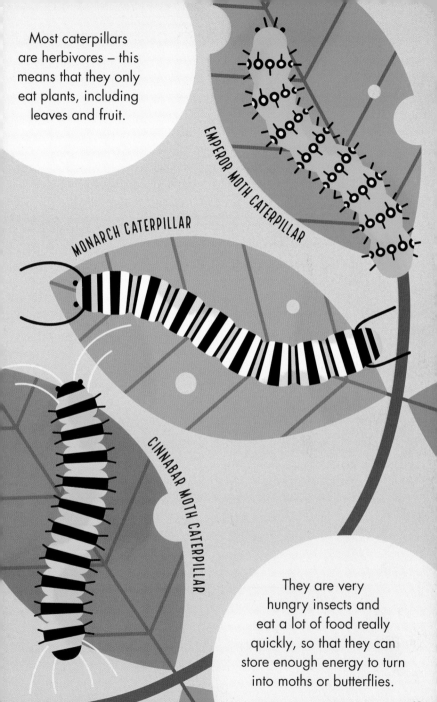

Most caterpillars are herbivores – this means that they only eat plants, including leaves and fruit.

EMPEROR MOTH CATERPILLAR

MONARCH CATERPILLAR

CINNABAR MOTH CATERPILLAR

They are very hungry insects and eat a lot of food really quickly, so that they can store enough energy to turn into moths or butterflies.

BUTTERFLIES

Butterflies are beautiful, but they're very shy.
To get a closer look, you can attract them
to your garden by laying out a fruity treat –
they love mashed banana!

Butterflies can
smell sweet
food with their
antennae and
with their feet!

PAINTED LADY
BUTTERFLY

PEACOCK BUTTERFLY

LARGE WHITE
BUTTERFLY

There are
around 12–15,000
species of butterfly.
And new species are
being discovered
all the time.

MONARCH BUTTERFLY

Butterflies have scaly wings. There may be 200–600 scales on every square millimetre of wing.

COMMON BLUE BUTTERFLY

RED ADMIRAL BUTTERFLY

MAGNIFY THIS!

Butterflies have a long tongue called a proboscis. They use it like a drinking straw as they feed, and coil it under their head once they've finished.

27

MOTHS

Although they look quite similar, it's easy to tell the difference between a butterfly and a moth. In the UK, butterflies are active during the daytime and moths usually come out at night.

CINNABAR MOTH

GARDEN TIGER MOTH

Moths aren't usually as bright as butterflies. They have furry bodies and are often brown, grey or white, but some types are very colourful.

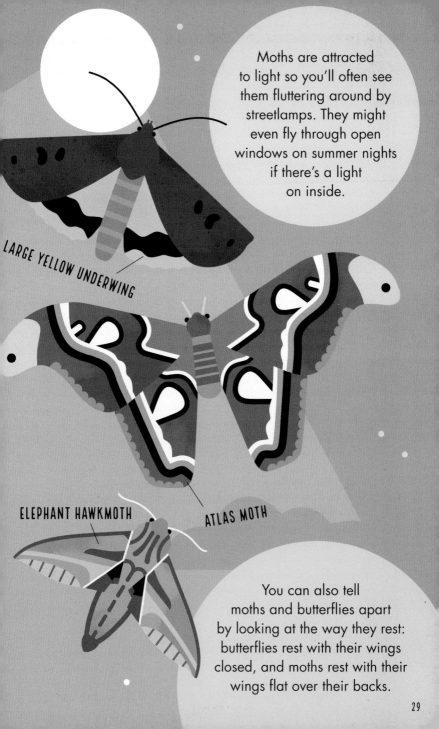

Moths are attracted to light so you'll often see them fluttering around by streetlamps. They might even fly through open windows on summer nights if there's a light on inside.

LARGE YELLOW UNDERWING

ELEPHANT HAWKMOTH

ATLAS MOTH

You can also tell moths and butterflies apart by looking at the way they rest: butterflies rest with their wings closed, and moths rest with their wings flat over their backs.

BEES

There are about 20,000 different species of bee in the world, and they're very important when it comes to helping things grow. Bees are very busy – in fact, they never sleep! They buzz around plants spreading pollen from one plant to another. This is called pollination and it helps many flowering plants to make seeds to grow into new plants.

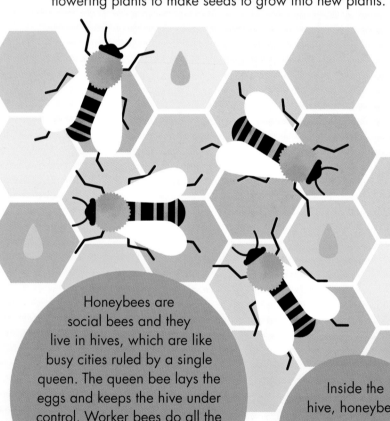

Honeybees are social bees and they live in hives, which are like busy cities ruled by a single queen. The queen bee lays the eggs and keeps the hive under control. Worker bees do all the rest. They build the nest, look after the young bee grubs and leave the hive to look for food.

Inside the hive, honeybees turn nectar into honey, which they store in honeycomb made of wax.

Bumblebees are also social and live in colonies, but not all bees do. Some are solitary and mostly live alone. Bees are not aggressive, but they can sting if they get upset so, to be safe, always keep your distance.

BUMBLEBEE

HONEYBEE

CARPENTER BEE

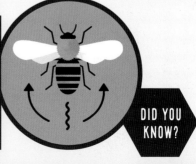

When a honeybee finds a patch of flowers, it returns to the hive and does a special dance to let the other bees know where the flowers are.

DID YOU KNOW?

WASPS

From a distance, you might get confused between bees and wasps, but if you get closer, there are some easy ways to identify them.

Bees have furry bodies and are usually gentle, whereas wasps can sometimes be aggressive. Unlike bees, wasps can sting more than once, so avoid them.

COMMON WASP

HORNET

SPIDER-HUNTING WASP

Most wasps don't survive through winter. For social wasps that live in colonies, usually only the queen comes out of hibernation in spring, ready to start a new colony.

DID YOU KNOW?

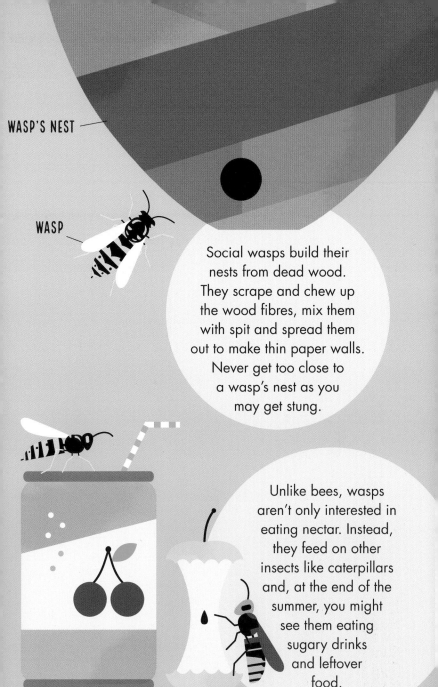

WASP'S NEST

WASP

Social wasps build their nests from dead wood. They scrape and chew up the wood fibres, mix them with spit and spread them out to make thin paper walls. Never get too close to a wasp's nest as you may get stung.

Unlike bees, wasps aren't only interested in eating nectar. Instead, they feed on other insects like caterpillars and, at the end of the summer, you might see them eating sugary drinks and leftover food.

33

ANTS

Ants are very hard-working insects that live in large colonies in almost every habitat around the world. Look out for them scurrying around the garden from spring to autumn, but less so during winter when it's cold.

Ants have very bad eyesight, but an excellent sense of smell. Wherever they walk, they leave a trail of scent so they don't get lost.

Like bees and wasps, ant colonies have a queen ant and worker ants. They all have different jobs to do – some ants defend the nest, some find food and some are involved in reproduction.

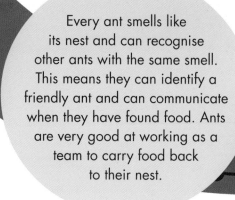

Every ant smells like
its nest and can recognise
other ants with the same smell.
This means they can identify a
friendly ant and can communicate
when they have found food. Ants
are very good at working as a
team to carry food back
to their nest.

DID YOU
KNOW?

Some ants have wings. On
sunny days they leave the nest
to fly off and start nests of their
own. They make their nests in
the soil and under stones.

FLIES

Flies are some of the most common insects in the world – but they're also some of the most unpopular. They like to land on your food and buzz around the house, and some flies even bite.

Houseflies like to lay their eggs in horse and pig poo, which means they can spread germs with their feet. They like feeding on anything sweet and dribble on their food before they eat – so avoid eating anything that you've seen a fly land on.

HOUSEFLY

BLUEBOTTLE

Bluebottles can spread diseases because they like eating things that are dead or nearly dead. Their eggs hatch into wriggling white maggots.

CRANE FLY

Crane flies are sometimes called daddy-long-legs because they have unusually long legs. They are slow and much easier to catch than smaller flies.

HORSEFLY

Horseflies have very sharp mouthparts and a painful bite, which can cut skin and make it bleed.

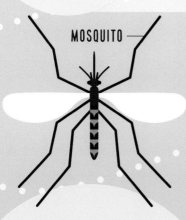

MOSQUITO

Mosquitoes like to suck blood and, although most types are harmless, some can spread diseases such as malaria.

COMMON GNAT

Gnats are very common insects, and you might be able to hear them humming as they fly around at night. They lay their eggs on the surface of water and hibernate through the winter.

37

FRESHWATER MINIBEASTS

Ponds and streams are fantastic places to look for minibeasts. There are all sorts of creatures that swim beneath the water's surface, and some that even skim across it. They are easy to catch with a net and, if you're quiet and patient, you can watch them come to the surface to breathe.

Pond skaters use their hairy, water-repellent feet and long legs to balance and skate across the surface of the water. They also use their short, stout front legs to pounce on other insects like mosquitoes that have fallen in.

WATER SCORPION

Sometimes these freshwater minibeasts are called bugs. Not all minibeasts are bugs though. A bug is a type of insect that has special mouthparts for piercing and sucking.

DID YOU KNOW?

You'll also find minibeasts under the surface of the water. Water boatmen (or common backswimmers) swim along on their backs and hunt for tadpoles, small fish and flying insects that fall into the water. They have wings, so they can fly from pond to pond when the weather is warm.

Water scorpions also have wings, but they rarely fly. You'll see them clinging to plants by the edge of the water. They breathe air while they're underwater by using spikes from their abdomen as snorkels!

— WATER BOATMAN

POND SKATER —

Be careful if you catch a water boatman because it may bite. And don't get water boatmen confused with lesser water boatmen – they swim on their front instead!

DRAGONFLIES AND DAMSELFLIES

If you're visiting a pond during the summer, you might also see dragonflies and damselflies zipping across the water. They start life at the bottom of a pond, as larvae or nymphs. After a year or two underwater, they climb to the surface where they shed their skin, unfold their wings and fly away to live as dragonflies (but not for very long, as most dragonflies live for less than three weeks).

EMPEROR DRAGONFLY LIFE CYCLE

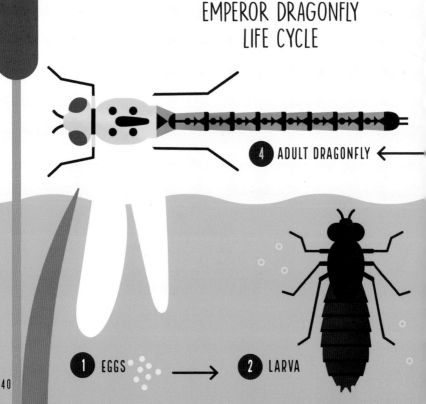

4 ADULT DRAGONFLY ←

1 EGGS → **2** LARVA

Dragonflies and damselflies lived before even the dinosaurs, but they were much bigger then – they were as big as seagulls!

You can easily tell the difference between dragonflies and damselflies. When dragonflies rest, their wings lie flat while damselflies fold up their wings instead.

COMMON BLUE DAMSELFLY

3 MOULTING

Damselflies have small eyes and a long, thin body, whereas dragonflies have a wider body and huge eyes – the largest of all insects!

APHIDS AND HARVESTMEN

Aphids, or greenfly, are one of the fastest breeding minibeasts in the world, and there are about 4,000 different types. The best time to find them is in spring and early summer. They'll be feeding near the tips of stems and under leaves.

Aphids' favourite plants are beans, fruit trees, potatoes and roses, and they feed by piercing holes in the stems of plants and sucking up the sap that pours out. Gardeners usually think of them as pests, because they also damage plants by passing viruses between them.

APHID

DID YOU KNOW?

Aphids make a sticky substance called honeydew, which ants like to collect for food. In return for drops of honeydew, ants protect aphids from predators, such as ladybirds and lacewings, by scurrying around and attacking any that come near.

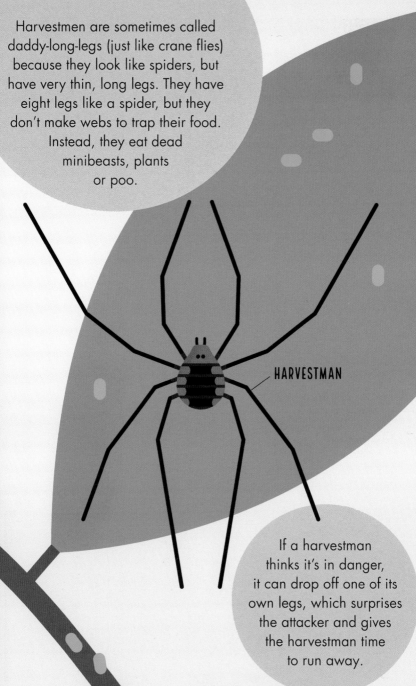

Harvestmen are sometimes called daddy-long-legs (just like crane flies) because they look like spiders, but have very thin, long legs. They have eight legs like a spider, but they don't make webs to trap their food. Instead, they eat dead minibeasts, plants or poo.

HARVESTMAN

If a harvestman thinks it's in danger, it can drop off one of its own legs, which surprises the attacker and gives the harvestman time to run away.

SPIDERS

Some people are scared of spiders, but spiders are also scared of people and they'll scuttle away if you get too close. To be safe, you should never pick up a spider with bare hands because some spiders have a dangerous bite or tiny hairs that can irritate your skin.

Spiders have eight legs, up to eight eyes, and bodies made of two parts – the thorax and the abdomen.

GRASS SPIDER

Spiders mostly eat insects and they are fantastic hunters. Some spiders stalk insects, while some trap them in webs made of silk, which the spider pulls out of nozzles on its bottom called spinnerets. Their webs are shiny, strong and very beautiful, and different spiders make different kinds of web.

All minibeasts with eight legs are called arachnids.

Sheet-web spiders start by spinning a silk sheet and then adding a tangle of fine silk strands above. The spider then hangs under the web and waits for insects to get tangled in the strands and fall into the sheet web.

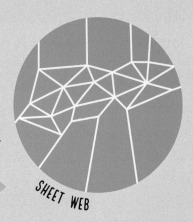

SHEET WEB

ORB WEB

Orb-web spiders spin webs with a patch of silk in the middle, where they wait to catch any insects.

Triangular webs have four spokes. The spider sits on a twig holding one of the lines to keep it pulled tight.

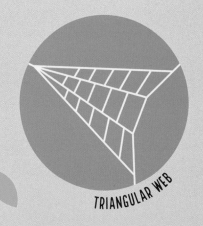

TRIANGULAR WEB

FUNNEL WEB

Funnel-web spiders make webs that spread out in a funnel shape from the middle. You'll often find these webs in corners or between stones.

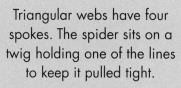

45

SPIDERS

When a minibeast gets stuck on a sticky spider's web it tries to wriggle free. This makes the web vibrate. Because spiders can't see very well, they sense the vibrations and rush across the web to grab their prey.

CRAB SPIDER

JUMPING SPIDER

Spiders have tiny mouths, so it's hard for them to chew their food. Instead, they squirt a liquid on to the trapped insect so it becomes soft. Then they suck up the juicy mixture and leave the dried out dead insect in the web.

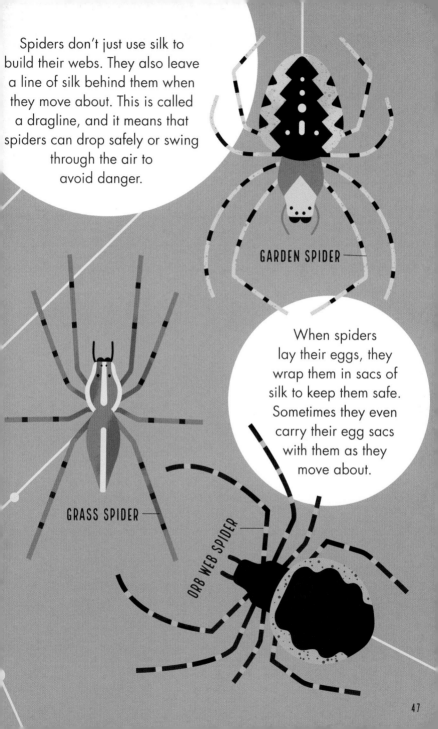

Spiders don't just use silk to build their webs. They also leave a line of silk behind them when they move about. This is called a dragline, and it means that spiders can drop safely or swing through the air to avoid danger.

GARDEN SPIDER

When spiders lay their eggs, they wrap them in sacs of silk to keep them safe. Sometimes they even carry their egg sacs with them as they move about.

GRASS SPIDER

ORB WEB SPIDER

SNAILS

If it has been raining, be extra careful when you're walking so you don't accidentally step on a snail. They love the wet ground, so look out for their big, round shells and soft, slimy bodies.

GARDEN SNAIL

BANDED SNAIL WITH A DARK LIP

Garden snails are very common and they can seal up their shell to stop their bodies from drying out.

MAGNIFY THIS! Snails have little eyes on the end of their feelers and they feed on plants.

LIP

BANDED SNAIL WITH PALE LIP

Most banded snails have spiral markings on their shells, but there are two types which are often confused. One has a pale lip and one has a dark lip, so you'll have to look closely to tell them apart. Their markings help to hide them from hungry birds.

49

SLUGS

Look out for slugs in rainy weather too. They look like snails, but without the hard shell. Slugs love damp cellars and wet corners of the garden, particularly sheds and outhouses where they can eat mouldy wood.

Slugs are covered in slime which helps them to move around – you'll notice their silvery, slimy trails in the garden and sometimes on windows. The slime trails also help them to find their way home as they each have their own scent.

GARDEN SLUG

Slugs have long feelers with eyes on the end and short feelers to help them smell. They breathe through a hole on their back and their blood is green!

MAGNIFY THIS!

LEOPARD SLUG

Both slugs and snails are known as gastropods, which means 'stomach foot' – this is because their slimy body is basically one muscular foot.

51

BEETLES

There are more types of beetle than any other creature on land and they come in all shapes and sizes. They live in all sorts of habitats, from hot deserts to polar ice caps, and you'll find them with many different colours and markings.

Click beetles live in flowers and on trees. If you hold one in the palm of your hand, it will pretend to be dead. Then it will flex its body quickly and throw itself into the air!

CLICK BEETLE

Soldier beetles are sometimes called 'bloodsuckers' but they won't really suck your blood. In fact, they are completely harmless to humans.

SOLDIER BEETLE

The cardinal beetle is bright red, so you'll find it easily on flowers or resting on tree trunks. Their antennae are long and feathery.

CARDINAL BEETLE

LADYBIRD

The ladybird is easy to recognise because of its spotty markings. Their bright red shell warns predators to stay away and they produce a smelly yellow liquid from their legs.

STAG BEETLE

Stag beetles are the biggest beetles in the UK and very rare. Males have large mouthparts called mandibles which they use to fight one another for females.

BEETLES

Cockchafer beetles come out at night and, like moths, they are attracted to light and sometimes crash into windows. They are sometimes called 'May bugs' because you'll notice them from May to August.

COCKCHAFER BEETLE

DEVIL'S COACH-HORSE

Bloody-nosed beetles get their name because, if they are attacked, they let out a red liquid from their mouth that tastes bitter and scares the predator away. Like most beetles, they are hard to spot because they are very secretive.

BLOODY-NOSED BEETLE

The devil's coach-horse also comes out at night to hunt for other insects, worms, spiders and slugs. To protect themselves from danger, they curl up their tail and squirt out a smelly liquid. Be careful if you find one because they bite.

55

MILLIPEDES AND CENTIPEDES

Millipedes and centipedes are both long and wriggly with many legs. They breathe through tiny holes in the sides of their bodies. Although they look similar, they have a few differences, which will help you to tell them apart.

Millipedes have between 40 and 750 legs, with two pairs of legs per body segment. Their legs are so strong that they can climb trees and even hang upside down, but they crawl along slowly instead of running fast like centipedes.

MILLIPEDE

Millipedes have rounder bodies and shorter antennae.

Centipedes have flat bodies, long antennae and they can run very fast. They have from 14 to over 300 legs, with a single pair of legs for each body segment.

COMMON CENTIPEDE

The legs at the front of its body are shorter than the ones at the back which means it never trips over.

Centipedes like to eat millipedes and other minibeasts, so millipedes sometimes hide by digging deep into the soil. Here, they eat dead plants and wood, and poo out fresh soil for new plants to grow in.

EARWIGS AND WOODLICE

Earwigs and woodlice love lurking in damp, dark places such as underneath logs or in cracks and crevices. Try lifting up a stone or log in the garden or park to see what scurries out.

Earwigs have pincers on the end of their abdomen. They use their pincers to fight with other earwigs, and to help them fold their wings back after flight.

EARWIG

Earwigs usually come out at night to hunt for dead plants, flowers and small insects to eat.

DID YOU KNOW?

If they are scared, some woodlice can roll up into a ball – just like a hedgehog!

WOODLOUSE

Woodlice have seven pairs of legs and a hard shell to keep their body safe.

Woodlice are in the same family as crabs and lobsters rather than insects, which means they need to stay damp to survive.

GRASSHOPPERS AND CRICKETS

There are almost 24,000 different species of grasshopper and cricket. As they grow, they shed their exoskeleton many times until they reach their adult form.

JUMP TO HERE

JUMP MORE THAN 20 TIMES THEIR OWN BODY LENGTH

As their name suggests, you'll find grasshoppers in grassy, sunny places. They can be brown, pink, purple, grey or black, but are usually green so they're camouflaged against the grass.

GRASSHOPPER

Grasshoppers have powerful legs. This means they can jump more than 20 times their own body length!

They rub their legs against their wings to make a chirruping sound, known as 'singing'.

Crickets have longer antennae than grasshoppers and usually only come out at dusk.

BUSH CRICKET

They 'sing' by rubbing their wings together instead of using their legs.

LACEWINGS AND COCKROACHES

Although lacewings and cockroaches are common insects, they're very difficult to see. Lacewings are almost transparent and cockroaches move very quickly.

LACEWING

Like many other minibeasts, lacewings come out at night and are attracted to light. They're often found near to farms because they eat insects like caterpillars and aphids, which like to munch on crops.

Their large wings have a lace-like pattern and sensors which detect ultrasound. This is a type of noise made by bats and means that lacewings can avoid being eaten by them.

Cockroaches are common minibeasts, but it's very unusual to see one. They only come out at night and are very fast to run away if they sense anyone around.

Even if a cockroach has its head cut off, it can live for up to nine days!

DID YOU KNOW?

They like to eat rubbish and rotting material and spread diseases, so don't touch a cockroach if you do come across one.

COCKROACH

EARTHWORMS

Earthworms are some of the most important minibeasts in the world because as they burrow through the soil, they mix it up and help plants to grow. Their bodies may look soft and squishy, but they are made of muscular and bristly body segments, which are perfect for squeezing through tunnels in the soil.

Worms can have more than one heart – some have five or even ten – and they can eat their own weight in food in a day!

EARTHWORM

Earthworms spend almost all of their lives underground. They usually only come to the surface on warm, damp nights in early summer when they are searching for a mate.

It's dangerous for worms to come to the surface because hungry birds and hedgehogs love to eat them.

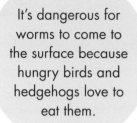

— HUNGRY BIRD

Worms don't have eyes, but their skin is very sensitive. If they feel a bird touching their tail, they can quickly try to get underground before the bird pulls them out.

MINIBEAST ACTIVITIES

You'll find minibeasts all around us (once you know where to look) and there are lots of activities you can do to get to know more about them. As many minibeasts are camouflaged, they can be hard to spot. However, there is an easy way to bring these minibeasts out into the open.

Set some minibeast traps in your garden by leaving half a grapefruit skin (open side placed downwards) near to some plants on a warm, wet day.

Leave it overnight and see whether any damp-loving minibeasts like slugs have been attracted to your trap.

1 Line a tray with a white piece of paper and place the tray underneath a leafy branch.

2 Gently tap the branch with a stick and any minibeasts hiding there will fall on to the paper where they will be easy to see.

3 You can then use a magnifying glass to get a close-up view of the insects as they scurry around.

Try using the tray under different plants so you can see where different minibeasts live. You can also try this by laying a white sheet on the ground.

MINIBEAST ACTIVITIES

To find freshwater minibeasts by a pond, you will need a net and a large bowl or shallow tray. It really is as simple as that. Remember to return all the animals to the water once you have finished looking at them. You can make your own net with a square of muslin, a stapler, a wire coat hanger, some pliers and a stick.

1 First fold over 6 cm along one edge of the cloth.

SQUARE OF MUSLIN

STAPLE HERE
↓

STAPLER

2 Staple down one edge to make a hem.

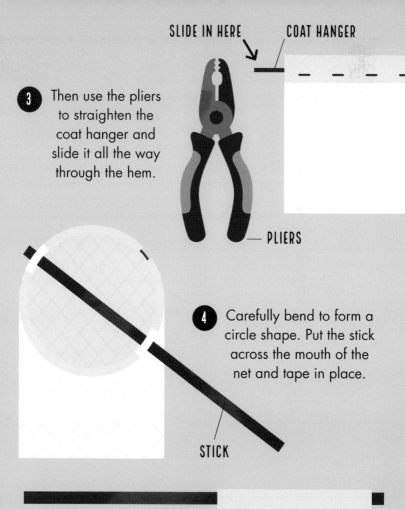

SLIDE IN HERE   **COAT HANGER**

3 Then use the pliers to straighten the coat hanger and slide it all the way through the hem.

— **PLIERS**

4 Carefully bend to form a circle shape. Put the stick across the mouth of the net and tape in place.

STICK

5 Finally, staple up the side and bottom of the net.

69

WHY ARE MINIBEASTS IMPORTANT?

Although some people think of creepy-crawlies as pests because they eat our crops and spread disease, minibeasts are an important part of life in every habitat.

Many creatures that live in leaf litter have a very important job to do, as they eat the dead leaves and trees – and some even eat dead animals and poo!

EARTHWORM

WOODLOUSE

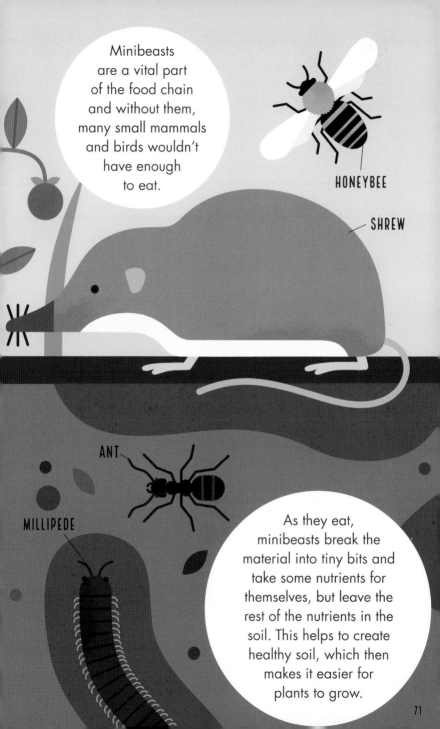

Minibeasts are a vital part of the food chain and without them, many small mammals and birds wouldn't have enough to eat.

HONEYBEE

SHREW

ANT

MILLIPEDE

As they eat, minibeasts break the material into tiny bits and take some nutrients for themselves, but leave the rest of the nutrients in the soil. This helps to create healthy soil, which then makes it easier for plants to grow.

71

MINIBEAST CLASSIFICATION CHART

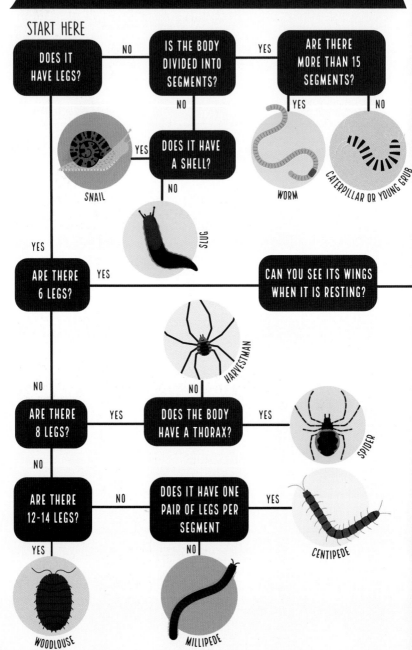

START HERE

DOES IT HAVE LEGS? — NO → **IS THE BODY DIVIDED INTO SEGMENTS?** — YES → **ARE THERE MORE THAN 15 SEGMENTS?**

IS THE BODY DIVIDED INTO SEGMENTS? — NO → **DOES IT HAVE A SHELL?**

DOES IT HAVE A SHELL? — YES → SNAIL

DOES IT HAVE A SHELL? — NO → SLUG

ARE THERE MORE THAN 15 SEGMENTS? — YES → WORM

ARE THERE MORE THAN 15 SEGMENTS? — NO → CATERPILLAR OR YOUNG GRUB

DOES IT HAVE LEGS? — YES → **ARE THERE 6 LEGS?**

ARE THERE 6 LEGS? — YES → **CAN YOU SEE ITS WINGS WHEN IT IS RESTING?**

ARE THERE 6 LEGS? — NO → **ARE THERE 8 LEGS?**

ARE THERE 8 LEGS? — YES → **DOES THE BODY HAVE A THORAX?**

DOES THE BODY HAVE A THORAX? — NO → HARVESTMAN

DOES THE BODY HAVE A THORAX? — YES → SPIDER

ARE THERE 8 LEGS? — NO → **ARE THERE 12-14 LEGS?**

ARE THERE 12-14 LEGS? — NO → **DOES IT HAVE ONE PAIR OF LEGS PER SEGMENT**

DOES IT HAVE ONE PAIR OF LEGS PER SEGMENT — YES → CENTIPEDE

DOES IT HAVE ONE PAIR OF LEGS PER SEGMENT — NO → MILLIPEDE

ARE THERE 12-14 LEGS? — YES → WOODLOUSE

72

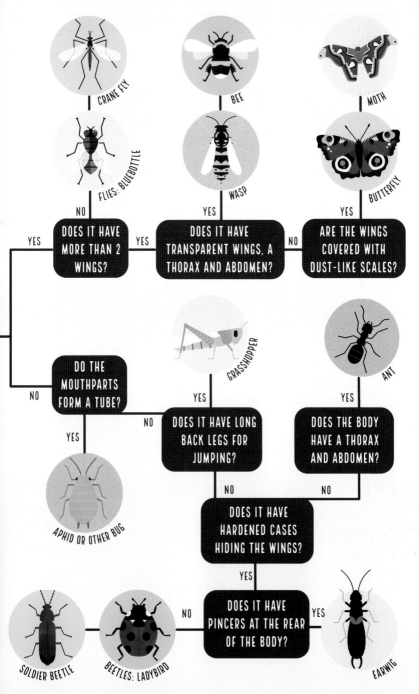

CRANE FLY

BEE

MOTH

FLIES: BLUEBOTTLE

WASP

BUTTERFLY

NO — DOES IT HAVE MORE THAN 2 WINGS? — YES

YES — DOES IT HAVE TRANSPARENT WINGS, A THORAX AND ABDOMEN? — NO

YES — ARE THE WINGS COVERED WITH DUST-LIKE SCALES?

YES

GRASSHOPPER

ANT

DO THE MOUTHPARTS FORM A TUBE?

NO

YES

NO — DOES IT HAVE LONG BACK LEGS FOR JUMPING? — YES

DOES THE BODY HAVE A THORAX AND ABDOMEN? — YES

APHID OR OTHER BUG

NO

NO

DOES IT HAVE HARDENED CASES HIDING THE WINGS?

YES

SOLDIER BEETLE

BEETLES: LADYBIRD

NO — DOES IT HAVE PINCERS AT THE REAR OF THE BODY? — YES

EARWIG

MINIBEAST SCALE GUIDE

You can find your favourite minibeasts here at the right size . . .

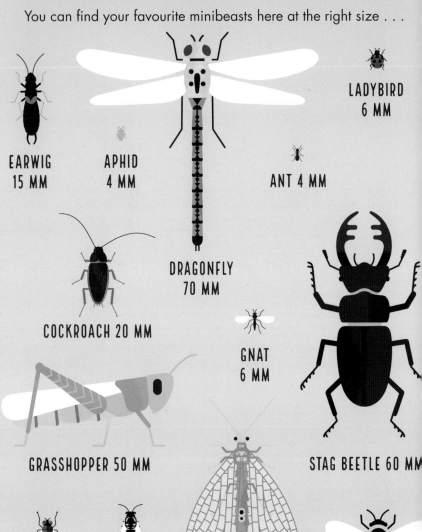

EARWIG
15 MM

APHID
4 MM

DRAGONFLY
70 MM

LADYBIRD
6 MM

ANT 4 MM

COCKROACH 20 MM

GNAT
6 MM

STAG BEETLE 60 MM

GRASSHOPPER 50 MM

BLUEBOTTLE
13 MM

WASP
15 MM

LACEWING 50 MM

BEE 20 MM

PAINTED LADY BUTTERFLY 70 MM WINGSPAN

CRANEFLY 50 MM

GARDEN TIGER MOTH 60 MM WINGSPAN

CARDINAL BEETLE
16 MM

HORSEFLY
20 MM

MOSQUITO
7 MM

SNAIL 30 MM

WOODLOUSE
10 MM

WATER BOATMAN
10 MM

WATER
SCORPION
20 MM

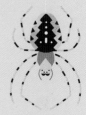

GARDEN
SPIDER
18 MM

MINIBEAST QUIZ

1. What is the name of the hard shell on the outside of a minibeast's body?
   - a. A skeleton
   - b. An exoskeleton
   - c. A proboscis

2. An insect has three parts to their body: head, thorax and . . . ?
   - a. Legs
   - b. Wings
   - c. Abdomen

3. What is a habitat?
   - a. Where a minibeast lives
   - b. What a minibeast eats
   - c. A net for catching minibeasts

4. What do omnivores eat?
   - a. Plants
   - b. Meat
   - c. Plants and meat

5. What type of minibeast has two sets of wings, with one set acting as a protective case over the other?
   - a. Lacewing
   - b. Dragonfly
   - c. Beetle

6. What is nectar?
    a.   Minibeast poo
    b.   A sugary liquid made by plants
    c.   A stage in a butterfly's life cycle

7. What is a baby bee called?
    a.   A nymph
    b.   A maggot
    c.   A grub

8. Which type of minibeast swims on their back?
    a.   Pondskater
    b.   Water boatman
    c.   Lesser water boatman

9. What are spiders' webs made from?
    a.   Silk
    b.   Cotton
    c.   Sap

10. Slugs and snails are gastropods, but what does that mean?
    a.   A 'slime tail'
    b.   A 'nose mouth'
    c.   A 'stomach foot'

GLOSSARY

ABDOMEN – The rear part of an insect's body, behind the head and thorax.

ANTENNAE – Feelers on the heads of many minibeasts, used to smell and find their way around.

ARACHNID – A minibeast with eight legs but no antennae or wings.

CAMOUFLAGE – The way that an animal's colour or markings help it to blend in with its surroundings.

CARNIVORE – An animal that kills and eats other animals.

CHRYSALIS – The hard case that protects a butterfly or moth pupa. Many moth chrysalises are formed within a cocoon of spun silk.

COLD-BLOODED – Animals that become hotter and colder depending on the temperature outside.

EXOSKELETON – A hard covering that supports and protects the bodies of some types of animals, particularly those without backbones, like minibeasts.

FORAGING – Wandering about searching for food.

GASTROPOD – A kind of animal such as slugs and snails that have one muscular foot. Most gastropods have eyes at the end of tentacles.

HABITAT – The natural home of a plant or an animal.

HERBIVORE – An animal that only eats plants.

LARVAE – The first stage of an insect's life cycle after hatching from an egg and followed by the chrysalis.

LEAF LITTER – Dead plant material that has fallen to the ground.

LENS – A clear part of the eye that focuses light to help see images clearly.

LIFE CYCLE – The stages a living thing goes through during its lifetime.

MANDIBLES – Mouthparts that are usually used for biting.

NECTAR – A sweet liquid produced by plants and used by bees to make honey.

NOCTURNAL – Active at night.

NYMPH – A young insect that is smaller than an adult and has undeveloped wings.

OMNIVORE – An animal that eats other animals and plants.

POLLEN – A fine powder made by plants to help them grow new plants.

PREDATOR – An animal that hunts other animals for food.

PREY – An animal hunted by other animals for food.

PROBOSCIS – A long, tube-like tongue, usually used for sucking or piercing.

PUPAE – An insect in a middle stage of development, after it is a larvae. Pupae do not eat or move, as they change into adults. This stage is also called the chrysalis.

RADULA – A flexible tongue with rows of teeth used by slugs and snails for feeding.

REPRODUCTION – When living things create offspring (babies).

SILK – Strong thread made by spiders and caterpillars.

SPECIES – A particular kind of animal or plant.

SPINNERETS – The part of a spider, insect or larva that spins a silk thread for its web or cocoon.

THORAX – The part of an insect's body that carries the wings and legs, behind the head and before the abdomen.

ULTRASOUND – A type of high-pitched sound that is too high for humans to hear.

INDEX